A Kalmus Classic Edition

ORCHESTRAL REPERTOIRE

COMPLETE PARTS
for

VIOLA

from the
CLASSIC MASTERPIECES

VOLUME IV

K 02196

CONTENTS

DIVERTIMENTO
K. 136 (Köch.Einst. 125a)
VIOLA
WOLFGANG AMADEUS MOZART
Allegro.

pizz.
arco
tr

Andante.
f
(p)
(mf)
(p)
(cresc.)
f
(mf)
f
(p)
(mf)
(p)
(cresc.)
f

Presto.

DIVERTIMENTO
K. 137 (Köch.Einst. 125b)

WOLFGANG AMADEUS MOZART

Allegro di molto.

Allegro assai.

DIVERTIMENTO
K. 138 (Köch.Einst. 125c)

WOLFGANG AMADEUS MOZART

Andante.
(p)
p
f p f p f p f
(cresc.)(mf dim. p)
cresc.
(_______ mf
dim.)
(p)
1. 2.

Presto.

CONCERTO GROSSO
Opus 6, No. 8

ARCANGELO CORELLI

Vivace
Vl. conc. I
p
Allegro
Vl. conc. I
p
f
p
f
p
f
p
f
1
p
f
p
f
p
Pastorale ad libitum
Largo
Vl. conc. I
p
f
p
f
Vl. conc. I
p
pp
f
p
pp

BRANDENBURG CONCERTO No. 3
in G Major
BWV 1048

JOHANN SEBASTIAN BACH

91
F
p
96
f
101
104
107
G
p
111
f
p
114
1
2
3
4
118
f
122
126
130
134
Adagio

Allegro
H
I
f
p

SERENADE
for String Orchestra
in C Major
Opus 48

PETER ILYICH TCHAIKOWSKY

I. Pezzo in forma di Sonatina

Andante non troppo (tempo del comincio)
275
ff
sempre marcatissimo
ff sf sf
fff
285
fff
sf sf sf sf
fff
II. Walzer
Moderato Tempo di Valse
Viol. I
pp
10
poco cresc.
rit.
mf
A a tempo
stringendo
rit.
20
3
5
3
Viol. I. II
pp
37
Viol. I. II
pp
45
più f
cresc.
mf
B
3
f
56
f
65
rit.
a tempo C
mf
75
cresc.
84
f
dim.
mf
93
cresc.

III. Élégie

Larghetto elegiaco
Poco più animato
pizz.
sempre p ma sensibile
più f
arco molto cantabile
cresc.
sempre cresc.
sf
mf
A
cresc. poco a poco
cresc. poco a poco
sempre cresc.
poco dim.

IV. Finale
(Tema Russo)

pizz.
arco
f
109
117
C
f cresc.
126
ff
136
Viol. II
ff
ff
143
D
ff
152
ff
159
166
E Vello.
Viol. I
f
176
Vello.
Viol. I
f
pp
186
poco a poco cresc.
196
F
Vello., C.-B.

323
332
L
f cresc.
343
Viol. II
ff
ff
7
ff
353
M
ff marcato
N
360
ff
368
376
384
Molto meno mosso
sf
fff
398
Viol. II
3 3 3 3 3
3
sf
ff marcatissimo
409
3
stringendo al - - - - - Tempo I
1
2
420
3 4 5
Più mosso
sempre fff
430
440

CONCERTO

for Two Violins
Opus 3, No. 8

I

ANTONIO VIVALDI

90
f
II
Larghetto e spiritoso
p
pp sempre
10
20
30
ppp
40
f

III
Allegro
spiccato e forte

CARMEN SUITE No. 1

GEORGES BIZET

No. 1. Prélude.

(Prelude to Act I)

E a tempo
smorz.
ppp
(♩ = 88.)
Andantino quasi Allegretto.
Nº 2. Intermezzo.
(Prelude to Act III)
pizz.
Arpa pp
A Arpa pizz.
1 Spieler
pp
Tutti
pizz.
p
cresc.
B
arco
f
dim.
p dim.
pp
smorz.
ppp
Cor. ingl.
pizz.
ppp
Nº 3. Seguedille.
(Act I)
Allegretto. (♩ = 160.)
pp
ppp
molto pp
A

36
rallent.
a tempo
B pizz.
pp
arco
C
f
p
sfz
p
sfz
ff
Nº 4. Les dragons d'Alcala.
Allegro moderato. (♩= 96.)
(Prelude to Act II)
pizz.
f
p
f
pp
A arco
pp
2
1
1
2 B Fag.I.pizz.
Fag.I.
pizz.
ff
3
5
Fag.I.
C pizz.
6
7
pp
arco
2 pizz.
pp
pppp

Nº 5. Les Toréadors.

(Introduction to Act I)

DOUBLE CONCERTO
in D Minor
BWV1043

JOHANN SEBASTIAN BACH

73
2 C
79
2
2
f
86
Largo ma non tanto
poco p
5
9
13
A
17
21
25
28
B
33

Allegro

LITTLE SUITE
Opus 1

II. Intermezzo.

f
p
mf
pp
div.
ff
1
p
cre _ _ _ scen _ _ _ do
1. pizz.
arco
f
p
p
C 2.
ff
3 3 3
3 3 3
p 3 3 3
3 3 3
3 3 3
3 3 3
div.
2
1
mf pizz.
D
1
2
1
cre _ _ _ scen _ _ _ _ do

f
arco
p
pizz.
pp
arco
p
E
mf
p
pizz.
p
div.
f arco
p
f
p
mf > pp < ff
fz
3
f
F
f sempre
di _ _ _ mi _ _ _ nu _ _
_ _ _ en _ _ _ do   f
dim. _ _ _ _ _ _ _ dim. _

G
pp
f
p
f
p
p
H
mf
mf
di -
di -
- - - mi - - nu - - en - - do f p
Flag.°
1
f
p
III. Finale.
Andante con moto. ♩ = 56.
Viol. II.
p
p
cre - - - scen -
A
- - - do f
di - mi -
Allegro con brio. ♩ = 80.
nu - en - do
molto
ff
B
p
1

f
di _ _ _ mi _ _ nu _ _ en _ do
C
p
mf
cre _ _ scen _ _ _ _ do
D
ff
Solo
fz fz fz p
E
2
pizz.
dim. pp
arco
f>

F
pp
cre
scen
do
f
G
cre
scen
do
sempre
cre
scen
do
ff
H
p
2

I
pizz.
cre _ _ _ scen _ _ _ do
f
p
arco J
mf
cre _ _ _ _ scen _ _ _ do
ff
fz fz fz
dim.
Più mosso.
pp
cre _ _ scen _ do ff

HOLBERG SUITE
Opus 40

EDVARD GRIEG

52
più f
fz
ff
ritard. al Fine
ff
ritard. al Fine
*) **)
ff
ffz
II. SARABANDE.
Andante.
p
p
p
cresc.
f
poco mosso
p
f
p
cresc.
mf
F 5
ritenuto poco a poco
Tempo I.
p
cresc.
f
ff
ritenuto poco a poco
Tempo I.
p
cresc.
f
ff
pp
cresc. molto
f
pp
cresc. molto
f
*) Absetzen. **) Bogenwechsel.

III. GAVOTTE.

MUSETTE.

Un poco più mosso.

IV. AIR.

Andante religioso.

V. RIGAUDON.

Allegro con brio.
SOLO.
TUTTI. fp
pizz.
f
cresc.
arco
pizz.
p
f
f
cresc.
T
cresc.
f
cresc.
piu p
p
piu p
U
pp
pp
TUTTI arco
ritard.
a tempo
Poco meno mosso.
ff
ff Fine.
p
mf
p
pp
f
V
p
cresc.
più tranquillo
rit. e dim.
ff
p
pp
Rigaudon da capo al Fine,
ma senza Ripetizione.